Believing Is Seeing

An Introduction to

The Power of Imagination

Andrew Wommack

Published in partnership between Andrew Wommack Ministries and Harrison House Publishers.

Woodland Park, CO 80863 – Shippensburg, PA 17257

ISBN 13 TP: 978-1-59548-650-9

For Worldwide Distribution, Printed in the USA

1 2 3 4 5 6 / 26 25 24

Contents

Introduction

Do you struggle to receive God's best for your life? Has the Lord called you to do something big, but you just can't see it for yourself? If you have trouble believing what God says about you, it's a problem in your imagination. One of the major things that changed in my life after the Lord told me I was limiting Him was that I began to change what I saw in my heart—my imagination.

On January 31, 2002, God spoke to me from Psalm 78:41 about my small thinking. I know that may sound simple, but it was a major block in my life. I've known since the Lord first touched my life in 1968, that I was called to something big. Within a very short period of time, I began to start having the desire to reach people all over the world with the Gospel and share the truths God was showing me. I knew God's will for my life, but that wasn't enough. I had to also see myself accomplish it.

Some people may think imagination is limited to fantasy, like imagining a talking mouse or a flying elephant. They think it's something children use during their play time and that adults, especially Christians, need to be more practical. Some Christians may also think using the imagination is just positive thinking.

Now, I'll admit, the definition of *imagination* can include fantasy, and in a sense, it involves positive thinking; but I'm not talking about those things. I'm talking about using your imagination to picture God's will for your life coming to pass.

In this booklet, I'm going to show you from Scripture that you actually use your imagination constantly. It's impossible not to imagine. You just have to deliberately choose to imagine the right things instead of the wrong things.

Your Imagination Sees

Where there is *no vision, the people perish: but he that keepeth the law, happy* is *he.*

Proverbs 29:18

The word *vision* means "a mental image produced by the imagination" (*American Heritage Dictionary*). So, you could say, "Where there is no imagination, the people perish." People are perishing for the lack of a positive imagination of what the Lord has in store for them.

The Amplified Bible says, *"Where there is no vision…the people are unrestrained."* Both the Darby Bible and English Standard Version say, *"the people cast off restraint."* That's because when people don't have any direction for their lives, they don't have any restraint. If you don't know where you are going, any road will get you there. But when you have a certain destination in mind, it limits which roads you can take.

Whether you realize it or not, you use your imagination every single day. For example, if you go to a store and park your car, you use your imagination to help you remember where the car is. When you are ready to leave the store, you will have a picture of that parking spot on the inside of you. It's not something you see with your physical eyes, but you can see internally where you parked. You remember if you have to go to the right or to the left. You remember how far away it is. You can picture these things. That's your imagination.

So, imagination is the ability to see with your mind what you cannot see with your physical eyes. It helps you see what can't be seen (2 Cor. 4:18). It creates pictures in your mind that help you remember, read, and plan. But imagination can only work with the information you give it—good or bad, right or wrong (Luke 6:45). If you fill your imagination with the trash of the world from movies, television programs, popular songs, and the internet, that's what it will produce. "Garbage in, garbage out," as the saying goes. But if you renew your mind to the truth of the Word, your imagination will help you receive from God (Rom. 12:2).

Most Christians don't have a clear vision for their lives. They cannot see God's will. But instead of seeking the Lord and engaging their imaginations, they let the circumstances of life push them around. Most Christians are driven by the "almighty dollar" just like unbelievers. They'll sometimes leave a good church and the support system of friends and family to move across the country just for a hundred-dollar raise.

They spend thousands of dollars on medicines that help them cope with sickness and disease. They mortgage their future to buy boats and other things they won't use and extra televisions they don't need. They settle for less than God's best because they are only looking at things with their physical eyes.

Vision—or the pictures of things produced in your imagination—gives you hope for the future. Without it, you'll never fulfill God's plan for your life. Circumstances will divert you, hardships will steal from you, and you'll quit. In the fifty-plus years since God called Jamie and me into the ministry, there have been many opportunities to quit.

We struggled, in part, because what we were seeing with our eyes didn't match the image we had on the inside. I knew in my heart, not long after the Lord touched my life in 1968, that we would have a worldwide ministry. But I wasn't experiencing it in my life, and my imagination wasn't as strong as it should have been. I just couldn't see myself doing it. There are a number of reasons for that, but once I took the limits off God and really started to see the things He had planned for this ministry, that's when it really took off.

Where Are Your Thoughts Going?

Thou wilt keep him *in perfect peace,* whose *mind*
is *stayed* on thee: *because he trusteth in thee.*

Isaiah 26:3

The word that was translated "mind" in this verse, is
the Hebrew word *yetser.*[1] This scripture clearly links our
peace to keeping our minds stayed on and trusting in
God. This reveals that our emotions follow our thoughts.
This is a major point that psychologists miss. They say
emotions are a result of circumstances. If that were so,
then everyone who has experienced the same negative
circumstances would have the same negative emotions.
But that's not true.

This exact same Hebrew word is also translated
imagination five different times in Scripture, including
in Genesis 6:5:

And GOD saw that the wickedness of man was
great in the earth, and that *every imagination of
the thoughts of his heart* was *only evil continually.*

The truth is your life is going in the direction of your dominant thoughts. You can't go anywhere in your physical body that you haven't already been in your mind. That's a huge statement!

You can actually create a self-fulfilling prophecy with your imagination. You might start to feel symptoms of sickness and then think about every worse-case scenario possible. It could even get to the point where you start mentally planning your funeral based on a twinge of pain, all because you let your imagination run wild— and your emotions follow!

Once, my board members sent me to the doctor for a stress test because of an insurance policy application. As the doctor began prepping me for the treadmill, his nurse asked if they could shave the hair off my chest to give the electrodes a place to stick. "You can't shave my chest," I said. "This is virgin hair. It's never been touched!" They tried to stick those things to my chest without shaving it, but about thirteen minutes into the test, they started falling off. In order to finish, I had to hold two electrodes in place, the nurse held two, and the doctor held two more.

When I finished running, the doctor looked over my results. Then he started grunting and writing on my chart. When he finally looked up at me, he said, "Here's the name of a doctor I know. He's a specialist. I want you to go over there and get tested right away. We might admit you into the hospital for open-heart surgery before the day is over."

The vast majority of people in this situation, including many Christians, would probably start thinking about the surgery, their loved ones, their funeral, their will, and everything they would miss out on if they died from a heart condition. That would be using the power of imagination in a negative way, but that's not how I responded. (We'll come back to this story later.)

How to Conceive a Miracle

The definition for *yetser* is "a form; figuratively, conception (i.e., purpose)."[1] I believe that your imagination is where you conceive things. And just as a woman has to conceive a child in her physical body, you have to conceive your miracle in your imagination. A stork doesn't deliver babies, and you don't just go to the hospital and receive a baby. You have to conceive a baby and then give birth.

Even though the Lord revealed to Abraham and Sarah that they would have a son (Gen. 18:9–14), God's will didn't automatically come to pass. There had to be a corresponding action to produce a child.

[Abraham] staggered not at the promise of God through unbelief; but was strong in faith, giving glory to God; And being fully persuaded that, what he had promised, he was able also to perform.

Romans 4:20–21

Through faith also Sara herself received strength to conceive seed, and was delivered of a child when she was past age, because she judged him faithful who had promised.

Hebrews 11:11

In a similar way, you conceive in your imagination what God wants you to do. Your imagination has miraculous power to conceive things. It is your spiritual womb.

Being born again, not of corruptible seed, but of incorruptible, by the word of God, which liveth and abideth for ever.

1 Peter 1:23

The Greek word for *seed* in the verse above is *spora*,[2] which is derived from the Greek word *sperma*.[3] It's saying that the Word of God is like a seed—a sperm—and it has to be planted in your heart to conceive—in your imagination.

So again, for you to conceive a miracle, you have to use your imagination. If it's foolish for a woman to just pray for a child but never have a physical relationship with a man, it is just as foolish for you to pray for healing but never see (imagine) yourself healed.

See with Your Inner Eyes

Years ago, I heard a story about a pastor's wife who had such poor eyesight she was legally blind. She had to wear very thick glasses to be able to see anything. Though she believed her husband's preaching about healing, she just wasn't able to experience it in her own life. No matter how many people prayed for her, she never saw the results she desired. The woman began to despair of never being able to see without her glasses. A healing evangelist was coming to their church, and she knew he would want to pray for her; but she had been disappointed so many times that she didn't want to go through that again. So, she avoided him until the very last night of the meeting.

He finally cornered her and asked if he could pray for her. He had her take off her glasses and then prayed a simple prayer of faith for her healing. After prayer he said, "Now, can you see?" She started to open her eyes, but he said, "Don't open your eyes." She was confused. How could she tell if she could see if she didn't open her eyes?

Then he asked her the second time if she could see. As she started to open her eyes, he told her again to keep her eyes shut. She obeyed but wondered what he was doing. She had to open her eyes before she could see.

Then the third time he asked this woman if she could see. As she started to open her eyes, he told her, "I'm not asking if you can see with your physical eyes. You have to see yourself seeing with your heart before you will be able to see with your eyes."

Finally understanding what the man was trying to tell her, the minister's wife kept her eyes closed and prayed in the Spirit.

After a few minutes, she said, "I can see it. "I can see myself seeing!"

"Open your eyes," he said.

The minister's wife slowly opened her eyes. Her vision was restored, and she could see!

If more of us understood this concept, we would get different results when we prayed. Instead, after we pray, we immediately open our eyes, check our wallets, and feel our bodies to see if something has happened. But miracles don't come from the outside; they come from the inside.

You cannot pray for healing while also planning your funeral. You have to use your imagination to see the Word at work in your life. Don't wait for a physical manifestation to verify that God's promises are true. Instead, see yourself walking in health, without pain or sickness.

In my situation, when the Lord showed me that I was limiting Him by my small thinking, I was not letting myself dream and think big. Now, I knew what God's will was, and I knew He had called me to have a worldwide ministry. But I wouldn't let myself see it.

I had to change the way I saw myself and begin to see how God saw me—imagining a worldwide ministry. Otherwise, none of it would have come to pass. You have to be convinced that you are who God says you are in His Word. When you know that what God says about you is true, then you can see yourself qualified to do what God has called you to do and see your dreams come to pass!

How God Sees You

And there came an angel of the LORD, and sat under an oak which was in Ophrah, that pertained unto Joash the Abi-ezrite: and his son Gideon threshed wheat by the winepress, to hide it from the Midianites. And the angel of the LORD appeared unto him, and said unto him, The LORD is with thee, thou mighty man of valour.

Judges 6:11–12

Gideon was a lot like many Christians; he didn't feel like he was qualified for what God called him to do. He was hiding from the Midianites when an angel of the Lord appeared and told him he was a *"mighty man of valour."* He couldn't believe it at first and had to have the Lord confirm it to him three times (Judg. 6:17, 36–37, 39).

"Mighty man of valour"—that's an odd way to refer to a man who was hiding from the Midianites. But the Lord doesn't see things the way we see. God looks on the inside, while people look on the outside (1 Sam 16:7b). Gideon was a mighty man of valor in his heart. He just didn't know it yet.

Notice the angel said, *"The LORD is with thee."* The Lord had chosen Gideon to deliver the Israelites from the hands of the Midianites. The angel told Gideon that the Lord was with *him*, but Gideon couldn't see that in his circumstances (v. 13):

> *And Gideon said unto him, Oh my Lord, if the LORD be with us, why then is all this befallen us? and where be all his miracles which our fathers told us of, saying, Did not the LORD bring us up*

from Egypt? but now the Lord hath forsaken us,
and delivered us into the hands of the Midianites.

We can't evaluate God's presence and personal blessing on us by just looking at our circumstances. We have to see with our hearts before we can see God's will come to pass with our eyes.

The deliverance of the Israelites from the Midianites was beyond human ability. Gideon was expressing that he couldn't do it by himself. That's good! Every godly leader needs to recognize that only God's power can accomplish His supernatural results. We have to come to the end of ourselves before we reach the beginning of God.

It's a long story, but the Spirit of God came upon Gideon, and 32,000 men from the tribes of Israel gathered with him to fight the Midianites and Amalekites. Already vastly outnumbered, God eventually winnowed his force down to 300 men. When Gideon sneaked into the enemy's camp and overheard two men speaking of a dream that prophesied Israel's victory (Judg. 7:13–15), all his doubts about what the angel of the Lord had said to him were removed. He acted in faith on what God had said and saw the victory with his spiritual eyes despite overwhelming odds in the physical realm.

Gideon and his army really didn't have to do much after that. They didn't kill the Midianites because the Midianites killed themselves. All Gideon and his men really did was blow trumpets, break pitchers, and shout. Gideon achieved one of the greatest military victories of all time with the remaining 300 men, yet he started out with no confidence. God saw Gideon as a mighty man of valor, but that's not how Gideon saw himself. It took time and supernatural experiences for Gideon to change the image on the inside. Likewise, God knows who you are and what your capabilities are because He created you. Will you see yourself the way He does?

Design Your Future

Back in the late 1990s, when the Lord started speaking to me about going on television, I got really excited. I began preparing myself by seeing the set of our television studio. I started drawing designs for a studio, even though we hadn't set a start date or hired anyone to help us.

When we finally hired Stephen Bransford to help launch the *Gospel Truth* program, he grabbed hold of the vision God had shown me, and all these years later, we are taking the Gospel farther and deeper than ever before. As of this writing, we have the potential to reach more than five billion people worldwide.

While we were working to bring the *Gospel Truth* to television, the Lord spoke to me and told me this was just the start of my ministry. And this was after I had been in ministry for over thirty years! If something would have happened and I would have died, I would have missed out on what He called me to do. That was both encouraging and discouraging at the same time.

It was discouraging because I spent all those years being trained in the "school of hard knocks" for the ministry God had called me to. On the other hand, it was encouraging because I had seen some great things happen during those years. So, if I was just starting my ministry, that meant it was only going to get better!

When we started on television, January 3, 2000, we came to a point where things were working nearly effortlessly. Before that time, it was a struggle. We were on the verge of disaster. It looked like our ministry could die at any moment. Then, all of a sudden, things just began to work.

There was an anointing that wasn't present before. People began responding to our message and our ministry. Over the next two years, our ministry doubled. Finally, there was light at the end of the tunnel—and it wasn't another train! We were going to make it. We were going to survive. We actually started seeing people's lives change. Although we'd had problems all the years before, we just didn't quit. We would have limited what God wanted to do in our lives if we had.

I used my imagination to bring forth what the Lord had shown me about going on television—and building on the vision for a worldwide ministry. But even though we were experiencing significant success, we still weren't taking hold of everything God had for us. I was seeing things with my imagination, but I was still limiting God through small thinking. It restricted the vision the Lord had for my life and our ministry.

It wasn't until the Lord spoke to me about two years later—on January 31, 2002—that I began to see exactly how much I was limiting Him. He spoke that to me through Psalms 78:41 which says,

Yea, they turned back and tempted God, and limited the Holy One of Israel.

I was limiting God through my small thinking. At the rate we were growing I wouldn't live long enough to see the whole vision the Lord had given me come to pass. Things had to accelerate and quickly.

It wasn't long thereafter that I pulled my ministry staff together and shared with them what the Lord had shown me. I told them, "I don't know how long it will take to change this image on the inside of me, but I am going to change." Because I started to harness the power of my imagination and allow myself to see the things the Lord had for this ministry, things started to change much quicker than I had anticipated.

See Yourself Prosperous

Now unto him that is able to do exceeding abundantly above all that we ask or think, according to the power that worketh in us.

Ephesians 3:20

I sat down and wrote a letter to our partners, sharing what the Lord had shown me. Because printing and mailing takes time, along with our partners' responses, we didn't expect to see a change in their giving for months. But something started happening in the supernatural realm. I was shocked how quickly my life changed. Within two weeks, things happened that showed me it was beyond my doing; it could only be attributed to God.

Not long after sharing with my staff, people started giving and our income increased dramatically. That was before my letter even reached our partners. It was before I had a chance to fully share with the public what the Lord had shown me!

For decades, we had struggled financially. Our ministry income ebbed and flowed, and many times we had to have a financial miracle just to stay afloat. After living this way for a long time, I made the decision in the mid-1990s to start meditating on what the Word of God says about finances. I took about a hundred scriptures on prosperity and studied and meditated on them for two years.

Then, not long after that, a minister who taught on and was experiencing prosperity came to our Bible college. I listened to what he had to say, hoping to learn something. But what I found out instead was that this minister was teaching things I had already been meditating on. It was like a lightbulb went off on the inside of me, and I could finally see it! It wasn't long before prosperity began to manifest in our ministry.

Until I got that revelation on prosperity, our meetings seemed to always end up within $5 to $10 of breaking even, which was about $10,000 at that time. I never minister anywhere because of money, but our ministry had been capped because I hadn't seen us being prosperous. After the Word of God came alive in my spirit and I began to see us being prosperous in my imagination, immediately things changed. At the next meeting, the offering came in at nearly $25,000! It was awesome!

So, in 2002, when I made the commitment to remove the limits off God and really let Him work through me and our ministry, it shouldn't have been a surprise that the Lord responded financially through our partners. It was as if there was a dam in the spiritual realm that had been blocking the supernatural flow of God; and when I began to change the image on the inside of me, all those restrictions I placed on our success were removed. That power for prosperity began working on the inside of me, and we saw a supernatural breakthrough in our ministry.

Develop a Picture

Back in the early years of this ministry, when we were struggling financially, I got into a situation where I owed my landlord some money. I told him I didn't have the rent payment, but he said I could work off the debt. He owned a photography studio and was about to lose his business because he was overextended. He had some people quit and couldn't do all the work himself. So, I got in there and I just started praying and believing God to develop pictures, even though I'd never done it before.

Because of that, I was able to prosper, and this man saw the blessing of God on my life. Even though I started out not knowing how to develop pictures, this man—who was a professional photographer—noticed how well I was doing after only working in his studio for a short time. As a matter of fact, he offered me a 50 percent share of his business only two months after I started. The man who owned the photo studio took portraits, so producing a good image was important.

It would have been wrong for me, as the developer, to take credit for this man's work. However, because I was helping him produce quality photographs, he wanted to reward me. As believers, we are called to minister the Gospel to others and do the works that Jesus did (John 14:12), and we'll prosper accordingly (Phil. 4:19). But if we get lifted up in pride and start self-promoting, that will actually block the flow of God's power.

When I left Childress, Texas, and prepared to move to Pritchett, Colorado, the owner of that photography studio asked me if I would train my replacement. So, the new guy came in, I told him all the things I knew, and he just blurted out, "How do you do this?" He panicked because he didn't really know how I did everything so well. I couldn't just claim that I had some great natural talent so, finally, I just had to tell him.

I said, "I pray in tongues and God tells me what to do, and that's how I do it." He said "Well, I don't pray in tongues!" I said, "I can tell you how to pray in tongues. I can pray with you so you can receive the baptism of the Holy Spirit." But that's where the training ended. I had no ability to develop photographs on my own. God's favor was on me, and I drew out of my imagination what I needed to see.

Someone who develops photos has to have the knack to see a picture correctly just by looking at a negative. They learn to adjust the settings for the right exposure and colors, and it's very subjective. From there, they select the best image and begin the process of putting it on paper for the rest of the world to see.

That's what we do with God's vision for our lives. At first, only He sees His plans for us. Then, as we use our imagination, we begin to see His plans and callings for ourselves. As we draw out of our imagination and fulfill those callings, the world begins to see it too. If we do it with the right heart, it will bring glory to God and magnify Him.

Remember the Word of the Lord

Back when the Lord was showing me that I needed to stop limiting Him, our Charis Bible College was in a period of significant growth. So much so that it was outgrowing the 14,600-square-foot facility in Colorado Springs that housed our ministry, television studio, and school.

During that time, my wife Jamie was handling the business of the ministry and looking for a new building. She found a 30,000-square-foot building while I was ministering overseas, so we went to look at it after I got back. Jamie said, "This ought to last us forever!" But in my heart, I knew that wasn't the case. God had changed my thinking. I thought, *Oh, no. My vision is much bigger than that.*

I was already seeing the picture for Charis Bible College that God had put on the inside of me. Just like when I was working in that photography studio, I was seeing what no one else could see and with my imagination, I was conceiving it. And it was developing!

In time, we actually ended up finding a building that was 110,000 square feet, but only part of it could be used for office space. We had to build out the rest of it for our ministry and Bible college. Renovations on that building estimated $3.2 million, and that was on top of the purchase price of $3.25 million, which was a big step for us at the time.

After we purchased the building, we tried to obtain a construction loan for the renovations. Initially, the lender guaranteed the loan. They said, "We wouldn't give you a loan for the building if we weren't planning to give you the construction loan," In other words, they thought we had good credit. But for nine months, we waited. And every time we asked our banker about the loan, he kept telling us we would get it "next week." It was a difficult situation and we needed to move forward with renovations, but they just wouldn't give us the money.

Finally, the banker said, "We'll just get a new appraisal and start the whole process over." All I could see was another nine months of delays. Something didn't seem right, so I started praying, and I remembered some things that the Lord had spoken to me two years earlier. Someone had given me a prophecy that I wouldn't need to take out a loan because I already had my own bank.

When the Holy Spirit brought that to my remembrance (John 14:26), I thought, *I have my own bank? Where is it?* Then I recalled the rest of the prophecy—my ministry partners would be my bank! Somehow or another I hadn't associated the prophecy with the building program.

At the rate our ministry was going at that time, it would have taken us more than a hundred years to come up with that kind of money! But I was only seeing things through my physical eyes. I was looking at our ministry's income relative to the perceived need. All I could see was that big, empty building and that banker telling me we needed to start over with that whole loan process.

If I had committed to renovating that building without taking out a loan, it could have killed our ministry. But God came through, and the Lord brought this prophecy back to me, saying, "I don't want you to take out a loan. I'm going to pay for this."

Eyes of Faith

And he answered, Fear not: for they that be *with us* are *more than they that* be *with them. And Elisha prayed, and said, LORD, I pray thee, open his eyes, that he may see. And the LORD*

*opened the eyes of the young man; and he saw:
and, behold, the mountain was full of horses and
chariots of fire round about Elisha.*

2 Kings 6:16–17

I believe that God originally created us with six
senses not five. Before their fall, Adam and Eve commu-
nicated with God through their spirits. When Genesis
3:7 says that their eyes were opened, it isn't talking about
the eyes of their heart. It's talking about their physical
eyesight. They had been walking by faith (2 Cor. 5:7).
When they sinned, their spiritual eyes closed, and their
physical sight began to dominate them.

They were created with a sixth sense of faith. But once
they fell, their spiritual eyes closed, and their physical eyes
opened up to the existence that most of us live in now.
We're carnal, and we just go by what we see. But God
made man to be able to perceive things in the spirit realm.

In 2 Kings 6, there's an instance where Elisha was
surrounded by the Syrian host. His servant exclaimed,
"Alas, my master! how shall we do?" (2 Kgs. 6:15). Elisha
prayed and said, *"Lord, I pray thee, open [the young
man's] eyes, that he may see."* (v. 17). He wasn't talking

about his physical eyes. His physical eyes were probably already as big as saucers looking at all of the enemy troops surrounding them. Elisha was praying that his servant's spiritual eyes would be opened. All of a sudden, this young man saw with his heart and perceived all the defending angels.

This was the opposite of what happened with Adam and Eve. Their spiritual eyes dimmed, and they started being dominated by their physical sight. But Elisha's servant had his physical sight give way to being able to see with his heart. This is what needs to happen to us so that our imagination can function properly.

When you're born again, you receive a calling from God that is beyond human ability. Most people say they are trying to find out what God wants them to do, but they are usually looking for something that they can do on their own. They pray, "God, you just point me in a direction, and I'll take it from there!" That is just a wrong attitude.

If you are doing something that you can accomplish by yourself, then I believe you haven't truly found God's will for your life. God has a plan for you that is bigger than anything you can do on your own. It's going to take His supernatural ability working through you to do it.

As a young man, I was an introvert. I couldn't look a person in the face and talk to them. One time, a man walking down the street said, "Good morning," and he was half a block past me before I could respond also with "Good morning." I remember, wondering, *What is wrong with me?* But now, through our *Gospel Truth* television program, God has me speaking to potentially billions of people every day. I'm doing something that was impossible for me to do on my own because I started to see things differently with my spiritual eyes. I saw myself looking into the television camera and speaking to people in their homes.

God is a supernatural God, and most of us are shooting way below His perfect will for our lives. We're aiming at nothing and hitting it every time. You need to see things differently. You need to have your eyes opened and your understanding enlightened so you can see the hope of His calling (Eph. 1:18).

Uncover God's Wisdom

That the God of our Lord Jesus Christ, the Father of glory, may give unto you the spirit of wisdom and revelation in the knowledge of him: the eyes of your understanding being enlightened; that ye may know what is the hope of his calling, and what the riches of the glory of his inheritance in the saints.

Ephesians 1:17–18

Renovating our building debt-free was a big decision. But once I had that desire (Ps. 37:4), I prayed about it and then let the peace of God rule in my heart (Col. 3:15). The decision was potentially disastrous for the future of our ministry, and we didn't have any evidence to suggest that we could raise $3.2 million. Still, I had peace about it. So, we decided to start the renovations without taking out a loan.

I had our builder put tape on the floor to mark the place where every wall, door, or hallway would be, and I spent hours every night after everybody was gone, walking around that space. In my imagination, I would see those walls; and I wouldn't let myself step over the tape.

I actually put five-gallon buckets on the floor and placed sheets of plywood on top of them to make a stage. I would stand on top of that platform and preach sermons in what would be our auditorium. In my imagination, I saw myself ministering to a room full of people. I know some of you think I'm weird for doing that, but I think you're weird not to use the imagination God has given you! It's where you conceive things!

Fourteen months later, we had that $3.2 million, the building was finished, and we moved in without the debt of a construction loan. It was one of the best decisions I have ever made.

Even though it was illogical, we did it because I had peace in my heart about it. God's supernatural provision came through for us. Once I saw it in my heart, I would have had to backslide from God for it not to come to pass.

See, you cannot get a revelation of something that doesn't already exist. The Greek word *apokalupsis*, translated "revelation" in Ephesians 1:17, means "disclosure." It is derived from the Greek word that means "to uncover." Paul wasn't praying for the Lord to give us anything new.

He was praying for us to receive a revelation of what is already ours. I just needed to draw out the resources that were already available, and it came through our partners.

Because I had a close relationship with God, I knew to seek His wisdom when it looked like we might not be able to move forward with renovations. He revealed things to me and enlightened my understanding with that prophecy about my partners being my bank. Through the saints of God, our ministry had access to riches that the bank didn't—and we didn't even have to pay interest! Amen!

Draw Out the Vision

Just a few years later, we were at capacity again in our new building. As I drove every day from my home in the mountains to our offices in Colorado Springs, I passed a particular property just outside Woodland Park, which is a bedroom community tucked away in the mountains near Pikes Peak.

What I didn't know is that about the same time the Lord was speaking to me about starting Charis Bible

College (early 1990s), the man who owned that property in Woodland Park had dedicated it to Christian education just before his death. (Visit **awmi.net/sanctuary** to watch the "History of the Sanctuary," which tells the miraculous story of how our Woodland Park campus came to be.)

We bought the property in 2009, but I had already seen the new campus of Charis Bible College in my imagination. I saw windows all across the front of a building so students and visitors could look out at Pikes Peak. Later, I met the family of that man, and they told me the Lord had revealed a similar vision to their father just before he died—nearly twenty years before!

At the time of this writing, there are buildings on our site that we built and acquired for more than $130 million above our normal operating expenses, and it's all debt-free. Praise the Lord!

In 2022, we broke the 1,000-student enrollment barrier at our Woodland Park campus. But we soon learned that about 500 more students would have come if we had had student housing available. That's about the time the Lord spoke to me about how I was limiting Him again.

So, I shared with our partners the vision for building a full campus, including housing for individual students and families, a student activities center, more classroom space, a media production building, a conference center and hotel, and more.

You see, these aren't my ideas. Through my relationship with God and my willingness to harness the power of imagination, the Lord placed the vision for all these Charis campus buildings *in my heart*. The vision was already in my born-again spirit, and through praying in the Spirit, I was able to draw them out.

Back when I was contemplating what to do with the bank and the loan for our former building in Colorado Springs, I committed to specifically set aside time with the Lord to pray. At the time, we lived on property with miles of trails that I had personally built. I took a walk down one of them and prayed in tongues to seek an interpretation. I wasn't a hundred yards down that trail before the Lord brought to remembrance the prophecy about my partners being my bank. (Over the years, I've discovered that God will show me solutions or answers through praying in tongues and interpretation.)

When you pray in tongues, it's your spirit praying. Your spirit has been born again, has the mind of Christ (1 Cor. 2:16), and knows exactly what to do. It has an unction (anointing) from God so that you know all things (1 John 2:20), and there is no limitation in your spirit. If you could walk in the power and revelation of your spirit, it would transform your physical life.

Take the Gospel Farther and Deeper

Once I started imagining God's plans for our ministry and seeing things with my spirit, we had a breakthrough with the second-largest Christian television network in America. Previously, our *Gospel Truth* program was only reaching 3 percent of homes in America. I was friends with the people who operated this network and had personally appeared on their show numerous times. But, for whatever reason, we just couldn't get on the network.

Then one day, not long after the Lord showed me that I was limiting Him, this couple contacted me and asked, "Why aren't you on our network?" They worked out the details that had kept us from getting on initially, and our program was on their network just one week later! Praise the Lord!

Since then, we've had numerous breakthroughs through television to where, as of this writing, we now have the potential to reach 5 billion people around the world in ten languages. That is more than half the world's total population! That's awesome! And there is no sign that we are going to be slowing down any time soon.

The Lord has put it on my heart to take the Gospel farther and deeper. That means we are working to expand the reach of this ministry and offer more resources to help people become discipled in the Word of God. Just on our website, awmi.net, we offer more than 200,000 hours of free teaching to help you build a stronger relationship with God and get to know Him better.

It wasn't long after the Lord touched my life on March 23, 1968, that I began to believe I would touch the world with the Gospel. But I didn't know how I would get from where I was to where God wanted me to be. The Lord just told me to sow the Word of God in my heart, so that I could put down roots. That way, when the time came for me to step into what He called me to do, I would be stable enough to handle the responsibility.

In the early years of this ministry, it didn't look like we would reach people all around the globe. People stayed away from our meetings by the thousands, and we struggled financially. If the Lord had really shown me back then what He had called me to do, I would not have been able to handle it. But as time has gone on, and I've grown in His Word, God has shown me more things. And as I have engaged my imagination, I've been able to draw them out of my born-again spirit.

See, you can't just microwave your miracles. There has to be evidence of growth before you reap your harvest. Jesus taught that *"the earth"* (likewise, your heart) brings forth "fruit of herself." But first comes *"the blade, then the ear, after that the full corn in the ear"* (Mark 4:28). Farmers can see their harvest in their imaginations, otherwise they'd never plant. But they also have to see that incremental growth in the physical realm before it's time to reap.

Maybe God has revealed the calling for your life, and you want to jump into it right away. But just like I had to see myself starting a Bible college, being on television, and then see building a debt-free campus, you have to see the steps God wants you to go take to get where He wants you to be. And if you are faithful and don't quit, you'll fulfill the calling God has for you (Gal. 6:9)!

Just Start Doing

But God hath chosen the foolish things of the world to confound the wise; and God hath chosen the weak things of the world to confound the things which are mighty; and base things of the world, and things which are despised, hath God chosen, yea, *and things which are not, to bring to nought things that are.*

1 Corinthians 1:27–28

When the Lord started talking to me about launching a Bible college, my first reaction was, "No!" But I had committed myself a long time ago to just do whatever the Lord called me to do. So I decided if I were going to start a Bible college, it was going to be different. We focused on discipleship and required our second-year students to take a mission trip.

Since then, we've added a number of third-year programs that focus on ministry, business, worship, film and production, practical government, leadership, and training students to start Charis campuses in other parts of the world. I wanted to know that our graduates would be sharing the Gospel globally and making a difference.

A good friend of mine visited our Charis Bible College and was very impressed. So, he decided to go back and start a Bible college in his own church. He sent me five pages of questions about how we do everything. The last question was, "If you had it to do all over again, what would you do differently?"

I thought a lot about that. When we started our Bible college, we did it on a shoestring budget because we had no money. I didn't have anybody to help me, and I didn't know what I was doing. But God knew who would go to school there, so it was important that we got started. We had to move forward and start developing God's vision for Charis in steps and stages. We had to walk before we could run.

One of our first graduates was a young woman named Carrie, who came from the small town of Kit

Carson, Colorado. When she came to visit our Bible college in the 1990s, it was in that 14,600-square-foot building that would seem tiny compared to the 650,000 sq. ft. Charis is at today. When Carrie first entered through the doors, the Lord told her that she would be connected with this ministry for the rest of her life. She graduated, went to Russia as a missionary, started a Charis campus there, put me on TV all around the Russian speaking world, got married, started a family, and then came back to Colorado sixteen years later to serve the ministry.

Today, Carrie Pickett and her husband Mike serve on my executive team and help operate our Charis Bible College's main campus here in Woodland Park, along with fifty-two other schools across the United States and around the world. Now, what if I had waited until everything was just right before I moved forward with what God called me to do? What would have happened to Mike and Carrie's calling?

We have learned a lot since Charis began, and there are a lot of things that we do differently now. But when God's called you to do something, you've got to get started even if everything isn't perfect. No one has ever been qualified to work for God, and you aren't going to be the first one. If you wait until everything in your life is totally perfect, you'll never do anything. If you feel foolish or weak, then you are just the person God is looking for. But you can't stay that way. You have to start seeing yourself the way God sees you!

See Yourself Blessed

My dad died from heart problems when he was in his early 50s. Because of that, the time I went in for a physical to qualify for insurance, the doctors projected my dad's problems onto me. They'll tell you genetics play a role in your health, so that's why they ask questions about your family history; but it seems like they are always thinking the worst. For example, they never account for my mother, who lived to be 96 years old. Surely, I'd have just as much chance to be as healthy as she was!

When the doctor gave me a serious diagnosis about my heart after my stress test, I was shocked! I didn't feel ill. The only reason I went to see the doctor was for an insurance policy. How could I need open-heart surgery? As I sat there for a second, looking at the doctor, I began thinking about the image of health and strength God's Word had painted on the inside me. And I said to him, "That's a lie. I don't believe it. You look at that readout again and tell me that it says I have a heart problem."

This reveals a big problem in the body of Christ. In church, we sing, "When we all get to heaven, what a day of rejoicing that will be," but if the doctor gives you a terminal diagnosis and tells you that you're headed there, you might fall apart like a two-dollar suitcase! You let your imagination accept the diagnosis by meditating on sickness and death. That is just wrong, wrong, wrong!

But I had spent a huge amount of time meditating on healing scriptures and reading things about Moses climbing Mt. Nebo the day he died—and he was 120 years old! Not only that, *"his eye was not dim, nor his natural force abated"* (Deut. 34:7).

So, the doctor just looked at me (probably because he wasn't used to people calling him a liar) and said, "Well, it doesn't really say you have a heart problem. It just says that there was an abnormality during testing. It may be nothing, but it could be something serious. We need to get you tested." He didn't think about the fact that those electrodes were falling off my chest!

"That's not what you told me," I said, getting mad. "You told me I might have to have open-heart surgery before the day is over. You lied to me!"

The doctor tore up the test results and said, "Fine! You're on your own! Get out of here!"

I had a nuclear stress test later, which was more accurate than a treadmill test, and was told that I had the heart of a seventeen-year-old.

See, what you ought to be saying in a situation like that is, "I believe I'm healed in Jesus' name, and this is going to be for the glory of God." Go to the Word for healing scriptures, and start seeing yourself healed from the sickness and walking in divine health the rest of your life. Amen!

Conclusion

Years ago, God showed me a vision of our life and ministry. In it, Jamie and I were pushing a huge boulder up a steep hill. It seemed like if we paused for even a moment to catch our breath and renew our strength, that boulder would just roll over the top of us. That's the way ministry had been for us for decades. If we had let up for even a moment, we would have been crushed.

Then, we went on television, and our ministry grew. Our income significantly increased, and we were able to pay bills. We weren't struggling any longer. The Lord showed me that it was as if Jamie and I had crested over the hill and were pushing that boulder on a plateau—on level ground. We didn't have to worry about how we were going to make it.

After that, the Lord showed me that at some point, we would start going downhill. In the vision, the boulder picked up speed, and we could barely keep up with it. I believe that's where our ministry is now because I have harnessed the power of imagination.

The Lord has shown me many things over the years, and even though I knew He had a plan for my life, I just couldn't see myself doing it. But we have to start seeing things with our spiritual eyes. We have got to start fulfilling the plans God has for the body of Christ.

I'll tell you; the Lord wants you to share in the visions He has for you more than you want to see them. He has given you an imagination to conceive those dreams and visions. And if you allow yourself to see them and remove all limits, nothing will be impossible with God!

FURTHER STUDY

If you enjoyed this booklet and would like to learn more about some of the things I've shared, I suggest my teachings:

- *The Power of Imagination*
- *Don't Limit God*
- *You've Already Got It!*
- *How to Find, Follow, and Fulfill God's Will*
- *10 Reasons It's Better to Have the Holy Spirit*

These teachings are available for free at **awmi.net**, or they can be purchased at **awmi.net/store**.

Receive Jesus as Your Savior

Choosing to receive Jesus Christ as your Lord and Savior is the most important decision you'll ever make!

God's Word promises, *"That if thou shalt confess with thy mouth the Lord Jesus, and shalt believe in thine heart that God hath raised him from the dead, thou shalt be saved. For with the heart man believeth unto righteousness; and with the mouth confession is made unto salvation"* (Rom. 10:9–10). *"For whosoever shall call upon the name of the Lord shall be saved"* (Rom. 10:13). By His grace, God has already done everything to provide salvation. Your part is simply to believe and receive.

Pray out loud: "Jesus, I acknowledge that I've sinned and need to receive what you did for the forgiveness of my sins. I confess that You are my Lord and Savior. I believe in my heart that God raised You from the dead. By faith in Your Word, I receive salvation now. Thank You for saving me."

49

The very moment you commit your life to Jesus Christ, the truth of His Word instantly comes to pass in your spirit. Now that you're born again, there's a brand-new you!

Please contact us and let us know that you've prayed to receive Jesus as your Savior. We'd like to send you some free materials to help you on your new journey. Call our Helpline: **719-635-1111** (available 24 hours a day, seven days a week) to speak to a staff member who is here to help you understand and grow in your new relationship with the Lord.

Welcome to your new life!

Receive the Holy Spirit

As His child, your loving heavenly Father wants to give you the supernatural power you need to live a new life. *"For every one that asketh receiveth; and he that seeketh findeth; and to him that knocketh it shall be opened…how much more shall* your *heavenly Father give the Holy Spirit to them that ask him?"* (Luke 11:10–13).

All you have to do is ask, believe, and receive! Pray this: "Father, I recognize my need for Your power to live a new life. Please fill me with Your Holy Spirit. By faith, I receive it right now. Thank You for baptizing me. Holy Spirit, You are welcome in my life."

Some syllables from a language you don't recognize will rise up from your heart to your mouth (1 Cor. 14:14). As you speak them out loud by faith, you're releasing

God's power from within and building yourself up in the spirit (1 Cor. 14:4). You can do this whenever and wherever you like.

It doesn't really matter whether you felt anything or not when you prayed to receive the Lord and His Spirit. If you believed in your heart that you received, then God's Word promises you did. *"Therefore I say unto you, What things soever ye desire, when ye pray, believe that ye receive* them, *and ye shall have* them" (Mark 11:24). God always honors His Word—believe it!

We would like to rejoice with you, pray with you, and answer any questions to help you understand more fully what has taken place in your life!

Please contact us to let us know that you've prayed to be filled with the Holy Spirit and to request the book *The New You & the Holy Spirit*. This book will explain in more detail about the benefits of being filled with the Holy Spirit and speaking in tongues. Call our Helpline: **719-635-1111** (available 24 hours a day, seven days a week).

Endnotes

1. Strong's Definitions, s.v. "יֵצֶר" ("yēer"). Accessed August 2, 2023, https://www.blueletterbible.org/lexicon/h3336/kjv/wlc/0-1/.

2. Blue Letter Bible, s.v. "σπορά" ("spora"). Accessed June 19, 2023, https://www.blueletterbible.org/lexicon/g4701/kjv/tr/0-1/.

3. Blue Letter Bible, s.v. "σπέρμα" ("sperma"). Accessed June 19, 2023, https://www.blueletterbible.org/lexicon/g4690/kjv/tr/0-1/.

Call for Prayer

If you need prayer for any reason, you can call our Helpline, 24 hours a day, seven days a week at **719-635-1111**. A trained prayer minister will answer your call and pray with you.

Every day, we receive testimonies of healings and other miracles from our Helpline, and we are ministering God's nearly-too-good-to-be-true message of the Gospel to more people than ever. So, I encourage you to call today!

About the Author

Andrew Wommack's life was forever changed the moment he encountered the supernatural love of God on March 23, 1968. As a renowned Bible teacher and author, Andrew has made it his mission to change the way the world sees God.

Andrew's vision is to go as far and deep with the Gospel as possible. His message goes far through the *Gospel Truth* television program, which is available to over half the world's population. The message goes deep through discipleship at Charis Bible College, headquartered in Woodland Park, Colorado. Founded in 1994, Charis has campuses across the United States and around the globe.

Andrew also has an extensive library of teaching materials in print, audio, and video. More than 200,000 hours of free teachings can be accessed at **awmi.net**.

Contact Information

Andrew Wommack Ministries, Inc.

PO Box 3333
Colorado Springs, CO 80934-3333
info@awmi.net
awmi.net

Helpline: 719-635-1111 (available 24/7)

Charis Bible College

info@charisbiblecollege.org
844-360-9577
CharisBibleCollege.org

For a complete list of all of our offices,
visit **awmi.net/contact-us**.

Connect with us on social media.

There's more on the website!

Discover FREE teachings, testimonies, and more by scanning the QR code.

Continue to grow in the Word of God! You'll be blessed!

Your monthly giving makes the greatest kingdom impact.

When you give, you make an impact in the kingdom that lasts for generations. Your generosity enables our phone ministers to answer calls 24/7. Your support is also expanding Charis Bible College and allowing *The Gospel Truth* to reach an even wider global audience. You do this and more through your giving each month!

Become a Grace Partner today!
Scan the QR code or call our Helpline at 719-635-1111 and select option five for Partnership.

Scace Partner today!

Andrew's
LIVING
COMMENTARY
BIBLE SOFTWARE

Andrew Wommack's *Living Commentary* Bible study software is a user-friendly, downloadable program. It's like reading the Bible with Andrew at your side, sharing his revelation with you verse by verse.

Main features:

- Bible study software with a grace-and-faith perspective
- Over 26,000 notes by Andrew on verses from Genesis through Revelation
- *Matthew Henry's Concise Commentary*
- 12 Bible versions
- 2 concordances: *Englishman's Concordance* and *Strong's Concordance*
- 2 dictionaries: *Collaborative International Dictionary* and *Holman's Dictionary*
- Atlas with biblical maps
- Bible and *Living Commentary* statistics
- Quick navigation, including history of verses
- Robust search capabilities (for the Bible and Andrew's notes)
- "Living" (i.e., constantly updated and expanding)
- Ability to create personal notes

Whether you're new to studying the Bible or a seasoned Bible scholar, you'll gain a deeper revelation of the Word from a grace-and-faith perspective.

Purchase Andrew's *Living Commentary* today at **awmi.net/living**, and grow in the Word with Andrew.

Item code: 8350

ANDREW
WOMMACK
MINISTRIES

CHARIS
BIBLE COLLEGE

God has more for you.

Are you longing to find your God-given purpose? At Charis
Bible College you will establish a firm foundation in the
Word of God and receive hands-on ministry experience to
find, follow, and **fulfill** your purpose.

**Scan the QR code for
a free Charis teaching!**

CharisBibleCollege.org
Admissions@awmcharis.com
(844) 360-9577

Change your life. **Change the world.**